A HISTORY AND DESCRIPTION OF

The Pitt Press

ERECTED TO THE MEMORY OF

Mᴿ PITT

FOR THE USE OF

THE UNIVERSITY PRINTING PRESS
A.D. 1833

ALTERED AND RESTORED
A.D. 1937

By E. A. CRUTCHLEY, M.A.

Cambridge
AT THE UNIVERSITY PRESS
1938

CAMBRIDGE UNIVERSITY PRESS
Cambridge, New York, Melbourne, Madrid, Cape Town,
Singapore, São Paulo, Delhi, Mexico City

Cambridge University Press
The Edinburgh Building, Cambridge CB2 8RU, UK

Published in the United States of America by Cambridge University Press, New York

www.cambridge.org
Information on this title: www.cambridge.org/9781107693395

First published 1938
First paperback edition 2012

A catalogue record for this publication is available from the British Library

ISBN 978-1-107-69339-5 Paperback

Cambridge University Press has no responsibility for the persistence or
accuracy of URLs for external or third-party internet websites referred to in
this publication, and does not guarantee that any content on such websites is,
or will remain, accurate or appropriate.

Author's Preface

THE chief sources for the history of the Pitt Building are the Syndicate minute books and other papers preserved at the Press, including much of the correspondence which passed at the time of the Building's conception and birth. Use has also been made of Mr S. C. Roberts's *History of the Cambridge University Press*, 1521–1921, Willis and Clark's *Architectural History of the University of Cambridge,* the *Cambridge Chronicle* and the *Cambridge Review.* A debt is due to many people who have supplied information from their memory of more recent times. Mrs J. B. Peace kindly lent the water-colour which is reproduced on the cover, and Mr E. B. Diver was instrumental in identifying the artist, whose initials are discernible (in the larger original, if not in the reproduction) on the cover of the wagon in the foreground. The copper plates engraved by Le Keux and Storer belong to Messrs Bowes and Bowes and are reproduced here with their permission.

Author's Preface

That the account compiled from such friendly assistance may win the approval of his readers is the humble and earnest desire of

THE AUTHOR

The University Press
New Year's Eve, 1937

Plates

1

UTTERING a prayer for one of Bellamy's pork pies (or according to another account for the state of the country he left) William Pitt the Younger passed away on 23 January 1806. Only thirty-three years before, a delicate boy of fifteen, he had come up as an undergraduate to Pembroke and had resided there, on and off, till 1780. He moved thence to chambers in London, entered Parliament in the following year, and in 1783 became, by the fortune of politics, England's youngest Prime Minister, before or since. A year later he was elected one of the Burgesses for the University, which he continued to represent till his death.

The impression his political character and ability had created was revealed by the growth of clubs in his name all over the country. The University Pitt Club at Cambridge, later than most, was founded in 1835. A monument to the "Great Commoner" was erected in Westminster Abbey at the State's expense, and another by the Common Council of London in the Guildhall. The proceeds of a subscription in Cambridge were used for the commission of a statue by Nollekens which was placed in the Senate House, and for establishing a University scholarship in his name.

As early as 1802 a public fund had been started to provide some national monument in his honour, but he asked that nothing should be done in this respect so long as he lived. The subscriptions were accordingly lodged with trustees to accumulate in the Public Funds. The task of arranging for their allotment eventually devolved upon the Committee of the Pitt Club of London, and it was decided to erect a statue by Chantrey in Hanover Square. A handsome sum still remained for disposal. The need for enlarging the premises of the University Press at Cambridge had been under discussion for some time, and it is Dr James Henry Monk (Bishop of Gloucester and Bristol, Professor of Greek from 1808 to 1823 and Bentley's biographer) who is credited with the suggestion that Mr Pitt's name should be associated with the extension proposed.

The Marquis Camden, Chairman of the London Pitt Club Committee, visited Cambridge and discussed the matter with the Vice-Chancellor, John Lamb, Master of Corpus Christi College. Subsequently he wrote a formal letter to Mr Lamb in the following terms:

Letter from Lord Camden

ARLINGTON STREET, *May 25th*, 1824.

Sir,

I have the Honor to inform you that I am just returned from a Meeting of the Committee appointed to consider of the disposal of the surplus of Money subscribed, many years ago, for the Erection of a Statue to the memory of Mr Pitt.

I am, now, authorized by that Committee to state to you, Sir, that which I had the Honor of personally communicating to you at Cambridge: "the disposition of that Committee to recommend to a general Meeting of Subscribers to the Fund above-mentioned the Disposal of a considerable Sum of Money for the Erection of an handsome Building connected with the University Press at Cambridge"; but, as it will be necessary to state to the general Meeting how far the University is disposed to find and provide a proper Scite for the erecting such Building, near or opposite to Pembroke College, I now trouble you on that subject, and I request you will have the goodness to inform me how far I may be authorized to inform the General Meeting of the Disposition of the University to find and provide a proper Scite as above-mentioned for the erecting of an handsome Building, which the Committee is desirous should be erected on such a scale as to be a distinguished Ornament to the University, and tend to perpetuate the Name and Memory of Mr Pitt.

I have the Honor to remain, Sir,

Your most obedient humble Servant,

CAMDEN.

P.S. The general meeting is appointed for the 11th of June.

There was no lack of a site, for in 1821 the University had bought from a certain James Nutter a piece of land which forms a considerable part of the present site of the Press. Before 1804 the works had been situated for a century and a half on the north side of Silver Street, on land bought from Queens' College and now belonging to St Catharine's. In that year it moved across the street where a warehouse had been erected some years before—the beginning of a gradual absorption of various properties lying between Silver Street, Trumpington Street, Mill Lane, and the river. So far as public houses are concerned, the process of expansion has been ruthless, no fewer than six having been cleared away.

The most notable of these was a part of Mr Nutter's messuage. The *Cardinal's Hat* or *Cap* faced on to Trumpington Street and was the first hostelry in the town encountered by travellers from London. Its frontage roughly corresponded with the central portion of the Pitt Building which replaced it, and it was no doubt this site which the University originally had in mind for the erection of a dignified entrance to the Press. The author of the article on the Press in the *Cambridge Portfolio* (1840) states that "Mr Pitt's Committee, at his *first* contested election, sat in a room at the Cardinal's Cap". He also records the popular saying of the time that "the intended tower to Mr Pitt's memory, by a singular coincidence, *would rise on the very spot whereon he first set his foot when he entered the University*".

A favourable answer having therefore been returned to Lord Camden's letter, a meeting of subscribers to the Fund was summoned by public advertisement to the Thatched House Tavern on 18 June 1824, with Lord Camden in the chair. There it was proposed by the Lord President of the Council, seconded by the Archbishop of Canterbury, and unanimously resolved "that the surplus of the Fund, after defraying the expense of the statue in Hanover Square, as re-solved at the former meeting on the 11th instant, be applied to the erection of a handsome and appropriate building at Cambridge, connected with the University Press; such building to bear the name of Mr Pitt". Lord Camden reported the decision of the subscribers to Mr Lamb.

"They feel", he wrote, "that it will be a most flattering addition to the character and reputation of Mr Pitt that his name should be connected with that Press from which emanate works of enlightened literature and profound science, and they trust they shall be enabled to add to the magnificent improvements now proceeding at Cambridge by the erection of a building which will adorn and decorate the University. They also trust that the University will feel a high degree of satisfaction in enrolling the name of Pitt among its benefactors, more especially as that eminent person mainly attributed his success in public life to his education within its precincts."

A Syndicate had been appointed in May 1824 "to consider what practicable improvements in the Town of Cambridge would be beneficial and ornamental to the University", and to this body the Senate referred the subject of the Pitt Memorial Building. It recommended that possession should be acquired of the houses on each side of the *Cardinal's Hat*, so that the proposed building might occupy the whole stretch along Trumpington Street between Silver Street and Mill Lane. A sum of £5000 was voted for this purpose, later increased by another grant of £3000. The purchases eventually cost a sum in the neighbourhood of £12,000 and were completed with some difficulty. It was not until 1831 that the last section of the site fell into the University's hands.

Probably on account of these delays the Committee deferred the preparation of plans until 1828, but in that year they approached seven architects and asked them to submit designs in accordance with the then available site. There is no record of the names of six of these seven, nor the nature of proposals, if any, they subsequently made. No doubt a Gothic conception was uppermost in the Committee's mind. Out of the architectural aspirations of eighteenth-century England, so wavering, confused, but marvellously ambitious, the new Gothicism had triumphed over its many rivals. Cambridge had resisted any inclination to dabble in the Moorish, Muscovite, or Chinese styles, and had accepted the pinnacles and mullions of Mr Wilkins and his peers with such enthusiasm that only financial stringency saved Gibbs's building in King's from similar encrustation.

Edward Blore was one of the protagonists of neo-Gothicism. His book on *The Monumental Remains of Noble and Eminent Persons* contains a number of his drawings, many of them engraved in steel by his own hand, and bears witness to his delight in Gothic form and detail no less than to his precious skill as an artist. His greatest monument is Abbotsford, which he designed and built for Scott. He was official architect successively to William IV and Victoria, and apart from a prolific output of new buildings, including some overseas, he carried out a great deal of restoration in cathedrals and churches all over the country. The Pitt Press is his only building in Cambridge. He was a little over forty years of age when the Committee invited him to submit drawings and finally chose him to carry out the work.

The selection made, Mr Blore travelled to Cambridge bearing a letter of introduction from Lord Camden to the Vice-Chancellor. The Superintendent of the Press, Mr Parker, had already met him in town to discuss the practical side of the undertaking. There was, of course, no question of such considerations interfering unduly with aesthetic ones, but the Committee, after stipulating "that an handsome room should be included in the design, together with a staircase leading to it", were obliging enough to grant that "any accommodation could be given to the Press in the building to be erected which did not interfere with those parts which they thought should be ornamented". On their side the Syndics were most amenable to the Committee's aims, abandoning a proposal for lodging rooms on the first and second floors so that the façade could be made uniform. They suggested that the pinnacles on the tower should be of one height (Mr Blore had shown the two towards the street being taller than the others) and they expressed some doubt about the lighting of the entrance hall. Otherwise they "all concurred in opinion as to the beauty of the elevation" which the architect had laid before them.

There followed consultations in Cambridge and London. Progress was held up while the University

Edward Blore

wrangled with the Corporation about the last two houses on the wider site. In March 1830 success seemed assured, and the architect was enjoined to make fresh drawings showing the proposed treatment of the wings, which it was hoped the University would soon be able to erect at its own cost. Mr Blore seems to have tired of the protracted negotiations. His new sketches were "so imperfect as to be almost unintelligible", so Dr Chafy, the then Vice-Chancellor, wrote to Lord Camden. "I would beg, therefore, to submit to your Lordship whether Mr Blore should not be directed by the Committee to furnish us with drawings in a more perfect and satisfactory state." Shortly afterwards Dr Chafy was able to inform the Committee that the house to the north of the block had at last come into the University's hands.

Lord Camden received this news "with great satisfaction". In view of the new state of affairs, the whole project was put up to fresh competition among the architects who had originally submitted plans, at which move Mr Blore justifiably took offence but was placated by Lord Camden. Ten months passed. Then, on 19 April 1831, the Syndicate formally approved Mr Blore's new drawings and a week later he was instructed by the Committee in London to proceed with the work. He estimated the cost of the central portion at £8000, leaving £1000 in the funds which he suggested should be used on the front of the wings, so that the whole façade might be the gift of the Committee. The remainder of the cost of the wings would be borne by the University.

That Mr Blore's new drawings were on the same lines as his original ones is suggested by the fact that he persisted in making the two west pinnacles of the tower lower than the others. It was not until after they had been erected that further protests resulted in their standardization, and in the final accounts presented to the Pitt Club Committee there is a charge for this alteration. It is doubtful how far the Syndics ever proposed to adopt the Pitt Building for the use of the Press itself. The large room stipulated by the Committee seems to have been intended for Syndicate meetings, and it had been allowed that, so long as the external effect was not sacrificed, the wings might be put to any practical use the Syndics chose. Mr Blore, at an early stage of the proceedings, spoke of a proposed warehouse on the Mill Lane corner, and the windows in the front of the building were so small that the wings can hardly have been meant for anything else but the warehousing of paper. This seems to be the only use to which they were ever put. Each had a doorway at the back of the building so that the central staircase could be avoided. One part of the building, adjoining the central block on the north, seems to have been set aside from the first as a dwelling-house, though there is no information about the early occupants.*

In any case, while the plans for the building were still under discussion, the Syndics decided upon a further extension of the Press premises, and Mr Blore was asked to furnish plans for the block which now forms the north side of the internal court, adjoining the Pitt Building at one end, and linking up at the other with the block which had been erected four years earlier. With a degree of melancholy which can only be imagined, Mr Blore abandoned the Gothic style and planned a brick building of Georgian aspect, matching its earlier neighbour. The cost was less than £1700. The new block backed on to houses along Silver Street, which were not removed for further extensions until the last few years of the century.

* Prior to the complete alteration of the building in 1936–7, it provided a service tenancy and latterly a home for the works caretaker, Mr Keetch.

2

IN the meantime building operations were begun on the central part of the Pitt Building. The ceremony of laying the first stone took place on 18 October 1831, and was attended by Lord Camden, Lord Farnborough and Henry Bankes Esquire, as representatives of the Pitt Club Committee, as well as by Lord Clarendon, Lord Harrowby, and the originator of the scheme, the Bishop of Gloucester. After an honorary degree had been conferred on Lord Camden in the Senate House, a procession formed and moved to the site. Here Mr Blore, Mr Walter (Clerk of the Works) and Mr Smith (the University Printer) conducted the visitors to their places. Coins of the reign (gold, silver and copper) were placed in a cavity in the foundation stone and covered up with a plate. Lord Camden, having completed the customary ritual of spreading the mortar with a silver trowel and testing the trueness of the stone with plumb-line and square, addressed the company in a manner which the *Cambridge Chronicle* of the time reported in the following terms:

The Foundation Ceremony

By the gracious permission of the University, and by the kind request of many friends, he had just experienced the high satisfaction of laying the first stone of this building, and he considered it as one of the proudest circumstances of his life to have been permitted to have that honour. From his heart he hoped and most cordially trusted that it would be the means of diffusing more generally that knowledge which the Press of Cambridge has hitherto been so pre-eminent in doing. He had formerly little thought that even the liberality of the University, or that the Funds subscribed, would have been so extensive as to have allowed a building which he hoped might vie with some of those ornaments with which the University had recently been adorned. In offering the funds to the University for the purpose, he looked not merely at the money obtained, but at the individual contributors, among whom would be found most of those who honoured and revered the memory of Mr Pitt; many of them were of the humbler classes, but there were also some of the highest dignitaries of the Church and Law, and many of the principal personages of the State, as, for example, the Hero of Waterloo, the venerable Earl of Eldon, the excellent and amiable Mr Wilberforce, and the venerable father of the present Chancellor of the Exchequer,* who lamented that his infirmities prevented him from attending on this occasion. Most earnestly did he hope that the undertaking might prosper, and that the knowledge diffused would be planted on the foundations of true religion, and of all those sciences for which this University has long been so distinguished.

* Viscount Althorp, whose father, Earl Spencer, had been a political supporter of Pitt.

The inscription on the stone, no longer to be traced, was as follows:

```
                 IN HONOREM
               GVLIELMI PITT
           HVJVS ACADEMIÆ OLIM ALVMNI
   VIRI ILLVSTRIORIS QVAM VT VLLO INDIGEAT PRÆCONIO
           ÆQVALES ET AMICI SVPERSTITES
   CVRATORES PECVNIARVM TVM AB IPSIS TVM AB ALIIS
             FAMÆ EJVS TVENDÆ
              ERGO COLLATARVM
       HOC ÆDIFICIVM EXTRVI VOLVERVNT
 LAPIDEM AVSPICALEM SOLENNIBVS CÆREMONIIS STATVIT
              VIR NOBILISSIMVS
    IOANNES JEFFRIES MARCHIO CAMDEN
 ASSISTENTIBVS EI HONORATISSIMIS COMITIBVS CLARENDON
               ET HARROWBY
   HONORABILI ADMODVM BARONE FARNBOROVGH
          HENRICO BANKES ARMIGERO
     TOTA INSPECTANTE ET PLAVDENTE ACADEMIA
   DECIMO QVINTO CAL NOVEMB ANNO M DCCC XXXI
    GEORGIO THACKERAY S T P COLL REGAL PRÆS
            ITERVM PROCANCELLARIO
```

A "sumptuous dinner" was held after the ceremony in King's Lodge, while all the individuals engaged on the Press, to the number of 120, were elsewhere regaled in commemoration of the event.

As the building proceeded a new character appeared on the scene—Mr George Peacock of Trinity College, afterwards Lowndean Professor and Dean of Ely. He was not a member of the Press Syndicate, nor of the Improvements Syndicate, but he had views on architecture and communicated freely with

Mr Blore.* After lamenting that "there is not a more unreserved intercourse between the Committee in London and the Syndics", he proceeded to criticize the building itself. In particular he condemned the proposal to leave the ends uncovered and expressed his willingness to raise amongst his friends the funds necessary to face them with stone. "There is a great objection to the use of brick in any public building of the University", he wrote. "You are certainly bound to limit yourself by your means, but I should think the Committee would not object to the additional expense being supplied by such means as I have mentioned. I feel very anxious about it for I know that if it is not done there will be a very strong expression of feeling about it." He offered to write to Lord Camden on the subject and eventually won his point.

He was less successful in his insistence that the side of the tower overlooking the court should be stuccoed. But he was able to procure various other alterations to the design, including the addition of

* At about the same time he wrote three pamphlets on the need for extending the University Library, and warmly supported Cockerell's design. He served on the Syndicates for building the new Observatory and the Fitzwilliam Museum, and after his appointment to Ely he not only persuaded the Chapter to undertake much-needed repairs to the Cathedral, but also secured the installation of an improved system of drainage in the city.

turrets at the ends of the gables of the wings, and the lowering of the pitch of the roof of the tower. In Mr Blore's original drawings this roof had been invisible, and he conceded to Mr Peacock's protests so far as to alter it to some extent. The effect, however, was still unsatisfactory: the roof obtruded itself upon the view from the road, and appeared to block the perforations of the balustrade. Mr Blore objected to making any further alterations and entered into some dispute with the Committee. Lord Farnborough agreed with Lord Camden that the architect should rectify the matter at his own expense. "Lord Farnborough is known to be a great protector of art and artists", Lord Camden wrote, "and I trust I am far from being illiberal to its professors, and we really both think that in such a case as this it would become you to make the roof of this building (which will do you great credit) as it ought to appear and as you meant that it should appear."

Whether Mr Blore eventually gave in and lowered the pitch of the roof still further, we do not know. Certainly it is still visible from the street and detracts a little from the ornamental effect of the balustrade. Nor do we know whether the architect was present at the opening ceremony on 28 April 1833. Dr Webb, Master of Clare and Vice-Chancellor for that year,

Mr Blore Indisposed

wrote to invite him. "I presume we shall have the pleasure of your company on that occasion. I shall be most happy to pay you every attention in my power and to show you how fully satisfied we are with your exertions on the building." Mr Blore, however, had been "attacked by the prevailing complaint" and could only promise to attend if his health permitted it.

3

THE deputation from the Pitt Fund Committee which journeyed to Cambridge for the ceremony of handing over the keys consisted of Lords Camden, Clarendon, Harrowby and Farnborough, Sir George Henry Rose, and Messrs Henry Bankes and Samuel Thornton. Honorary degrees were first conferred upon some of the party, after which the usual procession from the Senate House was formed. "Having arrived at the building", to quote from the account of the ceremony in the *Cambridge Chronicle,*

the Marquis Camden and the other noblemen proceeded into the grand entrance hall, and having invited the Vice-Chancellor to the door, his Lordship addressed the rev. gent. to the following effect: "Mr Vice-Chancellor and Gentlemen of the University of Cambridge: Whilst I place in your hands the key of this building, to be disposed of for the purposes for which it was erected as the University of Cambridge may now direct, I wish that it had fallen to some other of my friends and colleagues to address you upon this occasion, so interesting to us, and I trust, by the mode in which we are met by the University, equally interesting to them; but I do not pretend to deny that I have personally felt so much interest during the progress of this undertaking that I have the highest satisfaction in thus witnessing its conclusion.

THE PITT PRESS.

Lord Camden's Speech

"The idea of connecting the name of Mr Pitt with the Press of the University to which he owed his education and so much of his fame, was met by all parties with zeal and enthusiasm. The University have displayed an activity and liberality in providing this magnificent site which could only have been prompted by an admiration for the character of Mr Pitt. The Committee, animated by a personal respect and affection towards their contemporary, have endeavoured to cause to be erected on this site, such a building as might prove an addition to the other great improvements already perfected in this place, and which, from its peculiar destination, will unite the name of Mr Pitt with all those works of religion, morality, and science, which will in future emanate from it, and diffuse throughout the world the connexion of his name with erudition and learning. The manner in which the University have met the efforts of that Committee of which I am the unworthy representative on this occasion, deserves their warmest acknowledgements, and, if it were necessary, imprints still more deeply their respect for the place of their education.

"Sir, you have caused this ceremony to be attended by all the undergraduates as well as by the dignitaries of the University. Let me call the peculiar attention of all to this ceremony, and allow me to impress on the undergraduates that we, Mr Pitt's contemporaries, have been witnesses of his uniting the closest study with the utmost cheerfulness, and, when not employed in solving the most abstruse problems, he has engaged the admiration of his friends and companions, by the liveliest sallies of wit and imagination. Let his example stimulate you to the greatest exertion during your residence in this place, so well calculated to provide for your instruction in every department of literature and science."

His Lordship then presented the key of the building to the

Vice-Chancellor, upon receiving which the rev. gent. said, "It is most gratifying to me, my Lord, to be the person upon whom devolves the honour of receiving at your lordship's hands the key which puts the University in possession of a building for which it is indebted to the kindness and liberality of yourself and your illustrious colleagues. Like that erected in our sister University, which bears the name of one of the greatest statesmen of former days, that of Clarendon, this is dedicated to the memory of him whose counsels upheld, and whose guidance preserved, this country amid the torrent of anarchy and infidelity which overwhelmed the neighbouring nations, raising it to a dignity and eminence which rendered it the refuge and sanctuary of religion and virtue. These were the principles which guided his policy; his loyalty to his king was founded upon his reverence for, and his duty to his God; for he felt that this kingdom could flourish only through the union of Church and State. What more appropriate monument then could be erected to the memory of Pitt than this building, the chief purpose and object of which is to send forth to the world the Word of God; and could he, with prophetic eye, when residing in yon neighbouring college, whose proudest boast is to number him amongst her sons— could he have beheld such a structure, bearing his name, raised for such a purpose, and erected by such friends, even his own eloquence would have scarce sufficed to express the feelings of his heart. My Lord, the edifice with which you have adorned this University, and the illustrious name it bears, will add a fresh stimulus to our exertions in the dissemination of truth, the extension of science, and the advancement of religious knowledge; and I humbly trust that nothing will ever issue from these walls but such works as may conduce to the furtherance of these important objects.

The Opening Ceremony

"My Lords and gentlemen, in the name of the University of Cambridge I beg most cordially to thank you for this building, which forms so noble an addition to those which are already the pride and ornament of this University, and for which we are indebted to the munificence of a long and splendid train of royal and illustrious benefactors."

At the conclusion of the Vice-Chancellor's speech, the deputation and a considerable number of members of the University passed through the entrance hall to an ante-room at the foot of the principle staircase, where a handsome printing press had been fixed for the occasion, in order to give the noble Marquis an opportunity of printing off a copy of the inscription upon vellum for his own preservation.*

The other members of the deputation did likewise, after which the whole party proceeded to the Oriel room and there partook of a cold collation provided by the Syndicate. There was a dinner in Clare that evening in honour of the deputation and another in Trinity next day. In the following year the Duke of Gloucester's death left the Chancellorship of the University vacant. The election of Lord Camden as his successor may have resulted from the gratitude felt for the part he had played in these negotiations.

Various artists paid their tribute to the building.

* We may safely dismiss as spurious an alternative version of the inscription reported in *Punch in Cambridge*, a contemporary weekly of obvious political leanings: "This Building was erected at the expense of the London Pitt Club, gratefully to record the manifold blessings conferred by that great minister on his political friends, and on this University in particular."

The water-colour which serves as a frontispiece to this book was painted by George Belton Moore, and shows some shields carved on the stone panel above the front door which, though apparently intended at the time, were either abandoned or overlooked.* Of the two drawings reproduced opposite page 14 the top one is by F. Mackenzie from a lithograph prepared for distribution at the opening ceremony and probably made from the architect's sketches. The bottom one, by Challis, appeared in the *Cambridge Almanack*. Storer's version and another drawing by Mackenzie, engraved by Le Keux, face pages 18 and 24 respectively. R. B. Harraden also made a drawing, inferior to the others, which was engraved by Smart.

The finished building appears on the whole to have won the admiration of University and Town. An unidentified artist was instructed to engrave a vignette of the façade, and this was ordered henceforth to be introduced into the title-pages of all books with the imprint "Printed at the Pitt Press" beneath it. Mr Parker was authorized to engage "a proper person" as a door-keeper. The new interest aroused in the Press caused such an irruption of visitors

* The University shield which appears there now, and the pieces of stone on each side of the door engraved with the words "University Press", were added at the time of the alterations in 1936-7.

that in 1835 a notice was issued limiting the hours of admission, and stipulating that strangers and persons *in statu pupillari* must in all cases be accompanied by a Master of Arts.

Two details remained incomplete at the time of opening—the railings and lamp-posts in front of the building. Mr Blore's design for the former was approved by the Syndics in 1832, but was not carried out at once. They were finally removed in 1929, at a time when a general interest in the railings in the town led to several removals or alterations.

The lamp-posts present a mystery. Mackenzie's lithograph, showing two of a massive build standing one at each corner of the pavement in front of the building, probably represents the architect's proposal. Despite this suggestion the Syndics, in 1834, agreed that "four lamp-posts of the same pattern as those in the New Court of St John's College be erected in front of the Pitt Press", provided that the Commissioners for Paving and Lighting the Town, or the Contractor for Lighting, were willing to defray the cost. One such post, of Gothic tendency, stands to-day at the Mill Lane corner, but the other, facing Botolph Lane, is of simple design. The only evidence (there are no written records) that there were ever four posts is a picture of Trumpington Street by

J. M. Ince, reproduced in the *Cambridge Portfolio* of 1840 but possibly drawn some years before. Le Keux's engraving, with two posts in front of the door, may well be fictional, since other details in it are inaccurate. Storer's, however, published as early as 1837, shows the post facing Botolph Lane in its present position. It seems most probable that Ince was also portraying what he thought to be imminent, and that the authorities erected two Gothic standards, one of which, for some reason or other, was subsequently replaced.

Camden. Chancellor

F. Mackenzie.

J. Le Keux.

THE UNIVERSITY OR PITT PRESS.

4

IT has been seen that from the beginning the Syndics had probably no intention of using the wings of their new building as anything better than a warehouse, and they appear to have been only too glad to relegate the central rooms to other uses than those of the Printing Office. In 1832 Mr Whewell of Trinity had been granted permission to "appropriate for two years the two rooms on the ground and first floors of the Pitt Building as a temporary receptacle for the collection of minerals recently offered to the University by Mr Whewell, also for the Clarke collection formerly purchased by the University". In the year following the formal opening the Vice-Chancellor was allowed to suspend in the Pitt Press, until the Fitzwilliam Museum should be ready to receive them, the Mesman bequest of paintings, drawings and prints which the University had recently acquired. Later, the room on the ground floor was surrendered to the Professors of Greek for lectures, and subsequently to the Disney Professor of Archaeology "for so long as the Syndics think proper".

The Pitt Press

More significant was the provision of a home for the University Registrary. That official had moved from the ground floor of the "Public Library" to the Combination Room, King's College Old Court, in 1831. In 1836 the Syndics placed the ground floor room at the south end of the Pitt Press at his disposal. Twelve years later it was agreed "that the room in which the Syndics of the Press at present assemble* is more convenient for the purpose of their meetings than the room in the new building originally intended for them would be, and that the Syndics do not require such room for the use of the Press. And further that the Vice-Chancellor offer a Grace to the Senate to allow such room to be occupied as the Registrary's office in lieu of the room on the ground floor of the same building now used for that purpose." On 8 November 1848 the Registrary accordingly moved upstairs "to the noble room (built for the Press-Syndics-Room) in the tower of the Pitt Press"—so noted Joseph Romilly, Registrary at the time. There his successors remained, extending a little into either wing, for nearly one hundred years.

The Syndics' concern with the structure of the Pitt

* Probably on the ground floor of the 1826–7 building. This room was used by the Syndics prior to the erection of the present Syndicate Building in 1893.

Failure of the Staircase

Building by no means ended with its formal opening in 1833. A Minute of 19 May 1835 declared it expedient "that steps be immediately taken to put into proper condition the principal staircase in the Pitt Press, this staircase having failed to a great extent since it was erected in 1832", and "that the Vice-Chancellor be also requested to enquire whether any remedy could be obtained against any of the persons concerned in the original erection of the staircase". Mr Blore had been taxed on the subject and instructed the carpenter who put it up to report on the cause of the failure.

Swords had already been crossed over the failure of one of the floors of the block which Mr Blore had erected on the north side of the court adjoining the Pitt Building. It was alleged that the clerk of the works had advised him that his method of supporting this floor was insufficient but that the caution had been ignored; and the Syndics suggested that any expense incurred in remedying the fault should be borne by the architect. Mr Blore was hurt. He pointed out that a weight had been imposed on the floor which was six times as great as he had been told to expect. "As far as I am individually concerned", he wrote, "I cannot for a moment suppose that any disrespect could have been intended by a body of gentlemen from whom I have before experienced nothing but uniform kindness and attention."

In 1865 the stonework of the building itself began to show signs of deterioration. A provisional report stated that "the small pinnacles at the angles of the tower require immediate attention, being so perished by the weather that there is fear of a high wind blowing them off and endangering the lives of passers-by. The sill and mullions of the perforated parapet are also rapidly decaying." Another report added that "the chimneys in the tower next the back elevation are in a very dangerous condition", and as a result some £600 had to be expended on repairs. Ten years later cracks in the north wall of the tower were demanding attention.

The original stone used to face the building (it is not bonded to the walls but forms a coating about three inches deep) proved far too soft and has had to be replaced here and there at various times. Its insufficiency no doubt explains the loss of the foundation stone with its inscription. But the main peril through which the building passed cannot be brought home to the architect. Blame attaches itself to J. W. Clark, Registrary from 1891 to 1910, whose sturdy refusal to have his room disturbed by the inroads of sweeps led to an outbreak of fire in his

The Fire

chimney. The following account of the disaster is taken from the *Cambridge Chronicle* of 10 November 1893:

SERIOUS FIRE AT THE PITT PRESS.

About one o'clock on Wednesday afternoon, considerable alarm was caused by the sight of smoke and flames issuing from the top of the handsome tower of the Pitt Press. The "call" was at once given to the Fire Brigade, and the news spread rapidly through the town; in a very few minutes a crowd of some hundreds gathered round the scene of excitement. Meanwhile Mr Mason and the Pitt Press employees were busy getting to work with their appliances, which are kept in constant readiness for coping with such emergencies. Unfortunately, owing to the inaccessible position of the outbreak, some delay was caused before the hose could get to work, but with the assistance of Messrs Sindall's workmen, who are at present employed on the Syndicate buildings, the hose was hauled up the tower from the outside, and brought to bear upon the flames. The Brigade quickly arrived, and very soon some 25 or 30 firemen were on the spot. Captain Grey directed the efforts of the men, and under his guidance the fire was grappled with in a determined and business-like manner, which, together with the promptitude with which it was met, confined the fire to the top room of the tower. The room contained a large number of valuable printed books ready for binding. Fortunately a large number had been despatched to London only a few days previously, but a number of "Clarke's History of Cambridge", which are of great value, were utterly ruined.* In spite of the water

* The reference is probably to the *Architectural History of the University of Cambridge,* by R. Willis, revised and augmented by

thrown upon the flames, they had got such a firm hold that in a short time the roof fell in, and considerable alarm was felt lest the fire should spread to the Registrary's room, which is the second below the scene of the outbreak, and all energy was centred upon removing the invaluable documents contained therein. Great thanks are due to a number of members of the University, who rendered efficient service in effecting that object, and very soon all the papers were moved to a place of safety and the furniture was piled up on the staircase. The cause of the outbreak was said to have been the overheating of a flue, which is situated in the east corner of the tower on the Silver-street side, the stairs leading to the roof being the first part of the building ignited. Owing to the quantity of water used in quenching the flames the place was saturated; and as soon as the fire was got under, all attention was directed to removing the books and stationery stored in the rooms below. A body of police, under Supt. Innes, did good service in keeping back the public, and assisting the firemen. For some two hours the traffic in Trumpington-street was stopped, in order to give the men free scope, but by half-past three the fire was completely extinguished and the thoroughfare again opened.

The scene of the fire presented a most deplorable appearance, large piles of printed matter were saturated with water and charred by the flames, heaps of masonry work and burnt beams were covered here and there with the molten lead, the staircase which leads up to the room and which was continued up to the roof was burned and crumbling away. The damage done is very great, but no estimate can be given until the

J. W. Clark. The Press stock-books, however, have no record of the loss, and it is likely that the Registrary gave way, in a reporter's presence, to unjustified despair for the safety of his own work.

The Main Door and Entrance Hall

scene of the disaster is thoroughly overhauled and the books examined.

To avoid the danger of further outbreaks, a new chimney-stack was raised on the outside of the tower, built in stone and reaching above the roof on its north side. Two fire-proof rooms were also provided for Registry papers. In the meantime, Mr Clark took up a temporary abode in Pembroke College until his own room was ready again. Towards the end of his life, he struggled for the installation of a lift, but such a provision was not carried out during the Registrary's occupation.

The ecclesiastical appearance of the building, so deceptive to strangers, won for it the name of the "Freshman's Church", and was the cause of a warning in *The Fresher's Don't*: "Don't attend Divine Service in the Pitt Press. The music is not good."

5

T H E last forty years of the Pitt Building's history are uneventful. The Printer's persistent use of portions of the entrance hall as a dumping-ground for paper caused some friction, but, even so, the porchway served its proper purpose until 1919, when it was sacrificed to the Registrary's demands for increased space. The staircase was altered to provide an extra office on the ground floor, the hall was cleared, and a counter-desk was erected facing the front door, to be occupied by a clerk. A wooden porch with swing doors was built (in strictly Gothic style) inside the front door, to protect the clerk from the draughts and stares of the street. Access to the Press was diverted to the side entrances in Silver Street and Mill Lane.

In the summer of 1934 the new University Library was completed on a virgin site beyond the river, leaving the old buildings for transformation into lecture-rooms, department libraries, and offices for various University functionaries who had before been inconveniently scattered. The Registrary and his followers packed up their papers and forsook the Pitt

Building for new quarters. The musty rooms they had occupied for almost a hundred years were left temporarily derelict. Cupboard doors hung open, drawers leered their emptiness from all sides, clean unexpected squares of colour showed on the walls where pictures had been.

Mr John Murray Easton, the architect responsible for the alterations to the old Library, was charged by the Press Syndicate with the task of transforming Mr Blore's building into suitable offices for the printing department. For some years the Printer had been inadequately ensconced on the ground floor of the old Printer's house in Mill Lane, reached by an opening in the wall which had previously separated it from the works. Instead of a waiting-room, there was one upright chair in a dark corner of the office which would be hastily cleared of papers for the accommodation of visitors. If proofs or letters of past years were wanted, they had to be fetched from the cellars, or from the tower of the Pitt Building across the court. The office lay open to any incursion, and there, amid all the paraphernalia of ledgers and cost-sheets, clients were served, travellers inter-viewed, applicants for jobs examined.

All three floors of the Pitt Building, garbled by a century's improvisations, had to be replanned for its new functions. In a few months scaffolding began to rise inside and out. Some of the floors were found to be suffering from dry rot and had to be uprooted, so that at one stage the whole of the north wing was an empty shell. Mr Blore's staircase, already twisted out of its original course during the Registrary's occupation, was supplanted by a new one, winding round a lift on the other side of the tower block. Fresh stores of daylight were admitted by the widening of windows on the top two floors. A new, unrecognizable interior sprang up; cream walls—stairs, doors and bookshelves in natural oak—lights and fittings of contemporary design.

In June 1937, the Printer and his staff took up their new quarters. The square entrance hall, re-flagged with York stone, has a show-room on one side where recent publications are displayed. Facing it is a passage leading to the stair and lift, and a small waiting-room. On the first floor in the north wing, with a door through to the works, the Printer and his assistant have their rooms. The whole of the top floor is given over to offices and a library of books printed at Cambridge from the sixteenth century to the present day. On the north side another door leads into the works, and on the south a new bridge provides a link with the Secretary's department.

The Pitt Building To=day

The Altered Building

The ground and first floor of the south wing are given up to storage, and at the bottom of the north wing, reached from outside by a separate door, is a room for the use of the employees. In the tower itself three rooms, one above the other, are fitted for storage of letters and proofs.

The building, cleaned and partly refaced, presents an unfamiliar exterior to the passing world. In the *Cambridge Review*, while the transformation was in progress, an observer drew forgiving attention to the authorities' vandalism:

While London protests against the threatened destruction of one of Wren's least interesting churches let Cambridge not omit to lament the transformation of a familiar landmark which in its humbler way is not devoid of historical interest. Now that the University Library has gone to the Backs, and the Registry to the Old Schools, the Press in turn is preparing to re-occupy its old home on Trumpington Street. That gloomy building, erected by the Pitt Memorial Committee just over a hundred years ago, is one of the last survivors of an age when architecture aspired to be "sublime". Those towering walls with their minute and deep-set windows, that terrific tower with its cavernous portal and huge oriel, what are they but first cousins of Fonthill, more durable in construction, less fantastic in conception, but inspired by the same ideals of style? To-day large windows are being introduced into the upper floors, which change the emphasis of the building from vertical to horizontal; henceforward the sinister is tamed into the commonplace, and the architect's aims obscured....

The Pitt Press

A century's soot had possibly invested the building with an appealing grimness which Mr Blore can hardly have proposed. For all the change of emphasis caused by the wider windows, the "terrific tower", the "cavernous portal" and the "huge oriel" remain, even in Cambridge defying the epithet of "commonplace". The Pitt Press, its walls restored to the comparative whiteness which shone down on the distinguished company that spring day in 1833, probably better reflects the architect's vision now than it has for many a year past. It is the new interior which would have puzzled Mr Blore and his contemporaries most of all. As he looks out from his gilded frame in the Oriel room, does he pity or admire an age which has substituted its own complications of life and work for the extravagant artistry of his own?